T0159009

STROKE *to* HEELS

An encounter with God's restoring power

BOOKEY ITOANDON

authorHOUSE®

AuthorHouse™
1663 Liberty Drive
Bloomington, IN 47403
www.authorhouse.com
Phone: 1 (800) 839-8640

Published by AuthorHouse   09/27/2017

ISBN: 978-1-5462-0817-4 (sc)
ISBN: 978-1-5462-0816-7 (e)

Library of Congress Control Number: 2017914037

Print information available on the last page.

A gift for

_____

From

_____

on

_____

Message

_____

CONTENTS

Foreword...xv

Part 1

Chapter 1   First of All 1

Chapter 2   The Mind.. 9

Chapter 3   Controlled Mind-set 21

Part 2

Chapter 4   The Storm.. 33

Chapter 5   After the Storm...55

Part 3

Chapter 6   Expect Responsibility................................ 69

Chapter 7   All In.. 77

Part 4

Chapter 8   Pursuit of Me...91

Chapter 9   Not the End...107

About the Author...125

For Sweetie, Judah, and Jedidiah

and for my parents and siblings

for your love, support, and belief in me

Psalm 9:1(NLT)

I will praise you, Lord, with all my heart;

I will tell of all the marvelous things you have done.

Psalm 9:1(NLT)

I will praise you, Lord, with all my heart;

I will tell of all the marvelous things you have done.

FOREWORD

There are stages and phases in the journey of life. Some things work out as planned, others come out of left field. Nevertheless, while some things may be surprising to us, God is never surprised.

This book is a journey of faith written first hand from the author's point of view. It depicts her journey through self-realization and actualization and guides the reader through her experiences as an immigrant to the United States and the process of assimilation and integration. The dreams, challenges, life experiences and her walk of faith are nicely summarized. The turning point in the book is a life-changing event that challenged all she had believed, yet strengthened her faith. She became more resolute and secure in her faith and reorganized her life to have a greater purpose.

Some may have had similar pivotal moments in their lives, yet missed the opportunity for reflection. Others may not have had such an experience...yet, but can learn from the authors experience and take stock of their lives and purpose and realign their goals and efforts.

A quick read, this book can be easily completed and digested. It would impact your life.

Professor Oluyinka Olutoye
Pediatric Surgery
Texas Children's Hospital

PART 1

At first it may appear unreal, but with time it will all make sense.

CHAPTER 1

First of All

As human beings, we think we should be able to predict the results in our lives if we do the right things. For instance, if you study hard enough, you will pass the exam, or if you eat right and exercise, you will never get sick. I often wonder why and how we think we are in control when there is a God who created *all* things, who knows *all* things, and who can control *all* things.

How often do you go to bed with the thought that something will be wrong in the morning? No one wants that. We all pray for sweet dreams, sound sleep, and a bright morning.

We have certain routines we perform each night before bedtime. Perhaps you do some cleaning in the kitchen, wash your face, read a chapter or a page in a book, etc. One of mine is to pray with the family. We call it our prayer altar, and it consists of my husband, our darling boys, Jesus, and me.

However, I stay up longer to make sure the kitchen is tidy and maybe start preparing some things we'll need for the next day.

I believe no one goes to bed hoping something might go wrong with him or her or any loved one by morning. Instead, we go to bed hoping, believing, and trusting that the next morning will be much better than the previous. "Weeping may last through the night, but joy comes with the morning" (Ps. 30:5b NLT), especially when you have dotted all your i's and crossed all your t's to the best of your human ability.

If you are like me, who thinks everything has to be done in a certain way and always wants it done exactly that way, you'll think *yes*, you have all things under control—your children, your marriage, your husband, your business, ministry, and everything else that concerns you, and perhaps even a few that do not directly concern you. If something goes wrong in one or more of those areas, it will affect you. But when things are not going as smoothly as you'd like, you still have hope, knowing it's just a phase and that surely all will be well.

Well, that was me, and yes, I went to bed one night feeling good after a great meal, family prayer time, sending the boys off to bed, and spending some romantic time alone with my husband.

Alas, I woke up next morning feeling hale and hearty except for one thing: an unusual heavy feeling in my hand and leg when I got up to go to the bathroom.

At first I thought it was because of the gymnastics I had performed with my husband night before or perhaps because of the way I had slept; maybe I rolled over onto my arm while I was asleep. All sorts of normal causes came to mind, but none were related to illness.

Looking back at my life, from as far back as I can remember, I have mostly been aware and in control of things around me. That does not mean I respond to them all the time, but most times I have a clue of what it is going on and just pretend that I don't and not let it bother me.

Growing up in Lagos, Nigeria, I was sick with malaria most of the time. Because of the frequency of the illness, my parents didn't allow me to go to a boarding school, unlike my siblings. I was told by doctors that my sickliness was due to my blood genotype, AA, and that people with that genotype are prone to malaria (fever) and any stressful situation makes them sick.

But as an adult, after giving myself to Christ and studying His word, I have become aware of who I am in Christ and know that I am now a new creature and have been redeemed from sickness. "This means that anyone who belongs to Christ has become a new person. The old life is gone; a new life has begun" (2 Cor. 5:17 NLT).

After overcoming the roller coaster of illness, my health was very good until I relocated to the United States to join my husband and was diagnosed with a weak immune disease and placed on drugs. I traveled to Lagos, Nigeria, in 2010, six years after I moved to the United States but I had to cut my trip short and return immediately when a painful red rash appeared on my left shoulder and ached badly. I was told to apply mentholated talcum powder and that it was just a heat rash. But the pain became unbearable by the third day. That was when my husband changed my ticket so that I could return earlier than planned. From the airport, he took me straight to my doctor, who diagnosed the rash as shingles.

Now that my shingles outbreak, which left me with scars on my left shoulder, has been treated, I can't travel anywhere without being cleared by my doctor, who checks if there are any disease epidemics in my destination city or country before I embark.

But this great day—October 11, 2017—made the word of God clearer and more meaningful to me. Especially His word in Zechariah 4:6: "This is what the LORD says to Zerubbabel: It is not by force nor by strength, but by my Spirit, says the Lord of Heaven's Armies." There is no list of dos and don'ts to avoid life's problems. All the research and step-by-step guidelines out there are only suggestions to guide us toward healthy living, but there is nothing conclusive that can ensure a healthy life.

The only way, the only truth, of living to avoid and overcome illness and stroke is Jesus!

Whatever the mind can conceive and believe, the mind can achieve.

—Napoleon

CHAPTER 2

The Mind

The mind is shaped by whatever you feed it. A newborn baby is clueless of what is going on in his or her environment, but whatever you feed their minds forms who they are, who they will become, and what they believe. In a 2015 blog post by the University of Warwick, it says: "babies' minds begin to develop from birth, before they have language and before they begin to use autobiographical memory. Their interactions with their primary caregivers play an important role in developing their minds. So, who their caregiver is and whatever the caregiver says to them plays 80% role in their life."[1]

---

[1] Jane Barlow, "Babies in Mind and Why Parents Mind Matters," The University of Warwick: last revised mon 20 Jun 2016

The mind is a powerful object, and we should be careful what we feed it. What my caregivers fed my mind during childhood played a major role in what I did and became, until now.

I grew up in a Christian home with sisters and brother; we also had some relatives who lived with us. My parents raised us to live in love and taught us the way of the Lord.

My mom always told us to live as if we had no one to help us, to expect nothing from anyone; and that we just had to work and pray. I guess she formed that notion basically because she lost her mom at age six and was raised by her stepmom. So I grew up with that mind-set, that I had to work, work, work and figure things out for myself to make it in life. This shaped my life from childhood.

Margaret Boucher wrote, "The groundwork for your unconscious mind was laid in early childhood. What your parents said, how they acted and what you experience became embedded in your subconscious mind."

Eventually I went to college and gave my life to Christ, not because I was born into a Christian family and was just

going to church because my parents said so but because I fell in love with Jesus for me, by myself.

Then one day, while reading my Bible, I came across a scripture that said: "I can do all things through Christ who Strengthens me" (Phil. 4:13 NLT). This verse confirmed my motto growing up, that there is nothing on earth that I cannot do if I put my heart to it and pray. Because I read it in the Bible that I can do all things through Christ, who strengthens me (Phil. 4:13).

This scripture was embedded into my DNA: there is nothing I cannot do if I believe it, put my heart to it, and pray. These words became the main motivation for me to do and conquer things because I kept repeating them in my mind. Even when I am scared, I find myself saying, "I can do all things through Christ, who strengthens me."

This scripture became the basis for all that I do. Even when I'm tired, I keep telling myself, "Bookey! You can do all things."

I started doing business as far back as 1988, when I was in secondary school (known as high school in the United

States). My mom was an accountant at the National Bank Nigeria and also had a store where she sold provisions and some tailoring accessories. Her neighbor back then was a store that was used as a bakery depot. The bread depot closed early. As soon as all the bread baked for that day was distributed to different vendors, they left. I discovered that all through the day, people kept coming to my mom's store to ask for bread, and all we could tell them was that it was finished for the day.

I started learning how the vendors made their profits from collecting and selling the bread, and one day I told my mom I wanted to sell bread.

At first, she was reluctant. She said, "Your father won't allow it. You are not always here at the store." She was concerned because she had a store employee managing the store and wondered how I would keep up with my education. I explained to her what I had learned about how to calculate the commission and how to pay the bakery depot and how it wouldn't affect my school work. I also told her that I didn't like the way we turned people away after the

bakery employees were gone for the day. She finally agreed. That was how I started a business in high school; I believed I could do all things through Christ, who strengthens me.

In 1995, while studying law in college, I started a fashion business because of my friends' and colleagues' compliments about my tailored garments compared to their clothes, which they bought from big stores in Lagos or during their holiday travels outside the country. I have a very modest way of dressing, and I prefer to make my own clothes to suit my style. But I discovered that most people liked what I wore, and they started asking me how to get it. Well, I said to myself, "Wake up, girl! Here comes another avenue for you to make money." I was a solution to someone's problem.

I then met with my tailor and asked him to teach me how to measure. So the next time someone asked about my garments, I proudly announced it was made by me and if they were interested, I would measure them, charge for fabric and the sewing fee plus my profit, and make their desired garment. The business became so big that after I graduated from Nigerian law school during the 2000-2001, then I went to serve in the youth corps service. In Nigeria, youth corps service is similar to community service in the United States, but you are required to do it as a contribution to society. So while serving my community, I continued with the fashion business. Today, I have a fashion line called Attolle' Clothiers. Attolle is my indigenous name from Kwara State in Nigeria pronounced A-TO-LLE' meaning full and running over.

Even after I was hired at a law firm, I still made clothes. The fashion business grew so much that I started making shirts for bankers, both female and male, and some groomsmen. I also got contracted to make the uniform for the famous Big Mac fast-food stores with the head office in Maryland, Lagos, Nigeria.

In November 2003, I got married. I had planned to wait a year before starting a family because I wanted to spend the first year of marriage bonding with my husband, but as they say, man proposes, but God disposes. I became pregnant immediately.

In the fifth month of my pregnancy, I traveled to

London for vacation, and my husband joined me there. I went back to Nigeria after the two-week holiday, and he went back to the United States. Upon arriving home, I started processing my travel documents to the United States, and by May 2004, I left Nigeria for the United States to join my husband.

Upon my arrival in Houston, Texas, where he resided, the same drive I'd had from childhood, that I could do all things, came over me. I was now six months pregnant and in a new territory. My husband would leave for work in the morning and expect me to just relax with the baby and wait for him to get home. But I was too full of life and energy to just sit and watch TV all day.

I cleaned the house, cooked, and rearranged things. Maybe I should have written a book then, but the wifey role took over my mind, and I kept busy doing household chores like a new bride wanting to please her husband.

I could scrub the bathroom and kitchen floors without feeling any pain. I was so strong that I forgot I was pregnant sometimes. But my husband always got angry with me when he got home and found me cleaning and mopping the floor.

After the delivery of my first son, I entered college in Houston to study law. I dropped my baby off at the child-care center and went to my classes. While studying, I started a small business of buying items from the United States and sending them to Nigeria to sell.

In 2005, while I had all of this going on in my life, I decided to get a job. My first job in the United States was at Wachovia Bank. I got the job just to contribute because I didn't go to class every day and I started to feel empty. I had always been busy with one thing or another all my life; I'd never been lonely or not busy.

Anytime I started feeling empty, I found something to do, something to occupy my time and fill the vacuum, regardless of the task's importance or relevance at that moment in my life. I just couldn't be idle. My life had started becoming a restless one, unconsciously on my part.

My job at the bank went so well that I was given many awards for accomplishing goals and going beyond the set

standards. All this made me happy that I was fulfilling the scripture that says I can do all things through Christ, who strengthens me.

By the time I had my second son in 2007, I took time off for maternity leave and started contemplating changing jobs. After my maternity leave, I went back to work but quit my job a short time later. I didn't get a new job right away and decided to go help my husband at his office because I was bored and hated being idle. I had periodically helped in his office in the past, especially when it was busy, so we decided to work together. It also gave me more bonding time with my baby and kept him away from child care facility hassles.

This continued for three years, and by 2010, when both kids were in preschool, I decided to follow my real passion since childhood—fashion. Even though I was in a new territory and didn't know how to go about it, I believed there was somehow a way because *I could do all things*. That belief has shaped my mind-set and helped me to believe that I can do whatever I put my mind to.

The knowledge that you are what you think challenges you to think positively and treat every obstacle that comes your way as temporary. It's only a phase, and it will blow away like a season. If you are always thinking low of yourself, you will begin to see yourself only that way and become that way too.

If you believe staying away from those who hurt you, either intentionally or unintentionally, is the best way to live your life, you will gradually become the angry, unfriendly, moody, and proud type of person that you detest in others.

It's safe to pause at every detour we encounter on our life journey to reevaluate our vision, mission, goals, and purpose for doing things the way we do them.

The Mind is a powerful force.

It can enslave us or empower us

It can plunge us into the depths of Misery

Or take us to the heights of Ecstasy

Learn to use the power wisely.

—David Cuschieri

CHAPTER 3

Controlled Mind-set

Our thoughts and mind-set form the basis of what we do and what we become in life. Where you are today, the successes you've reached and the differences you've made are all connected to your mind-set. What you believe in your mind controls your unconscious thinking, your unconscious thinking controls your emotions, your emotions control your actions, and your actions produce your outcomes.

If you have a mind-set that one day you are going to write a book, for instance, that belief will take root in you, and as soon as you have an experience or go through an ordeal, you begin to feel (emotion) that you need to write it down for others to see, and that produces your outcome. These ideas formulate your core beliefs about life and how it works as well as your attitudes toward people and situations; therefore, they dictate the way you act in any situation, at any time. You will live your life using these beliefs as guidelines without even realizing it.

The mind is like a storage bin: you store away what you learn, experience, and see, and someday when a similar situation or circumstance presents itself, you dig those observations out, rearrange them, and make use of that information as they fit into the puzzle.

Once you believe it—though it might take a while— step-by-step, in every direction you go, you will find yourself moving toward your desired belief. No matter how long it takes, your mind-set will keep telling you that you can do it and that picture will remain in your mind, and if you don't quit, it will gradually come to pass.

What my parents and the passage of the bible that I held unto taught me used to control me, and unconsciously I refused to reevaluate what I believed or what I was doing. Gradually, I started to realize that I would agree to do something I did not feel like doing because I wanted to prove to myself and to others that I could do all things through Christ, who strengthened me. The pressure to prove that nothing was too hard for me kept mounting, and I continued to encourage myself in the Lord. After all, He said I could do *all*.

When I was in university in Lagos, Nigeria in West Africa, I took a class that registered only two students for the term. I chose that elective class because all my peers were running from the course, saying it was too complicated and that the lecturer was mean. So I dared myself to take the class and pass it very well on the first attempt because I knew I could do all things through Christ, who strengthens me. I took the class, and I passed it with flying colors.

At that stage of my life, I was enjoying all the results I was getting from using this particular scripture.

Little did I know that I had gradually shifted from doing things with God's help to doing them of my own power. My stubborn nature started creeping in. I just had to do whatever the task was, regardless what it would take.

This went on for so long, and human praise started

coming in too, which I believe made it worse. When people start showering you with praise for everything you do, watch out! That praise gradually creeps into your life and distracts you from the main purpose of what you are doing and why you are doing it. Those people don't know the reason behind your service, and you should never let their applause distract you.

Meanwhile, very few of those kind comments are real. Oftentimes, people just say things because they feel they have to. Either they feel that what you're doing is something they cannot do, or they wonder how you are doing it wholeheartedly and feel you need to be compensated.

They use kind comments as a form of compensation, not knowing that what you are doing is a covenant between you and God and has become second nature to you.

The mistake I made was to think I could handle it all without being distracted. But I got distracted big time. Tiredness, frustration, and stress started creeping in, but as a determined lady, I refused to admit to them. Instead, I made excuses and prayed when I was supposed to chill.

Stroke was a disease I used to think was caused by heart problems, especially blood pressure, which is linked to poor eating, smoking, and alcohol consumption. That's from my mind-set, which was controlled by the news.

If mind-sets can change us, maybe we can deliberately choose our mind-sets to improve our abilities. We can choose to adopt a mind-set that improves creativity, good deeds, and rest, for instance. When you become aware of all those mind-sets, positive or negative, which form the way you act or react to things in life, the best thing is to evaluate them and take steps to correct and delete the ones that are not profitable for you.

On August 5, 2010, I was involved in a fiery car accident on one Houston's major highways. It happened between 7:30 and 8:00 a.m. while I was on my way to drop off a sister in Christ. The traffic was initially moving slowly because of the morning rush hour, but by the time we moved out of traffic, I heard a loud sound, and I noticed the car wasn't stable. I decided to apply the brakes, and the car instantly started spinning in circles on the highway and then hit the road divider. It finally came to a stop, but by this time the fuel tank had caught fire. I turned to look at the lady beside me. She was already crying, like me, but through it all we were both screaming *Jesus!* We were able to unbuckle our seat belts, open the door, and run away from the fire.

By this time, we were already on the news, and my husband, whom I had left at home with our two boys, a six- and three-year-old, was already on the way to meet me. I had run out of the car without my shoes or purse, as I was in the habit of driving without shoes and putting my purse on the backseat. I was glad that my sister was with me and was able to come out with her purse, which she had placed on her lap during the ride. She called her dad first. He spoke to both of us. Then I called my husband, who confirmed that he had already seen it on the news and was heading toward us.

My thinking was to offer help as much as I could, but I learned that sometimes your heart wants to help but you do not have the capacity to carry it out. It is important to take time to calculate what an act of kindness will cost you to render rather than offer without thinking and then do it grudgingly. God loves a cheerful giver. "You must each decide in your heart how much to give. And don't give reluctantly or in response to pressure. 'For God loves a person who gives cheerfully'" (2 Cor. 9:7 NLT). I wasn't pressured into giving help in this situation; however, I decided to do it anyway. After all, my calculation of the distance and traffic involved had been wrong.

The mind and body are not separate; our thoughts have remarkable control over our bodies, and our mind-sets are capable of improving our brains' performance. An extremely important finding of Carol Dweck's long research into mind-set[2] that a person's mind-set is not necessarily permanent; mind-sets can be changed. We either have a fixed or growth mind-set. A fixed mind-set assumes that our character, intelligence, and creative ability are static givens that we can't change in any meaningful way and that success is the affirmation of that inherent intelligence. A growth mind-set thrives on challenge and sees failure not as evidence of unintelligence but as a heartening springboard

---

[2]   Carol Dweck, Mind of Achievement, www.mindsetonline.com.

for growth and for stretching our existing abilities. From these two mind-sets, which we manifest from a very early age, springs a great deal of our behavior, our relationship

with success and failure in both professional and personal contexts, and ultimately our capacity for happiness.

It's all up to you. If you believe you can, you're right, and if you believe you can't, you're right, too. Our minds are designed to be renewed. This is a proven scientific fact.

Romans 12:2 says, "Don't form your life around what the world says is right, but let God transform you into a new person by changing the way you think. Then you will learn to know God's will for you, which is good, pleasing, and perfect" (NLT).

How we respond to life's circumstances has an enormous impact on our mental and physical health. You might have not been able to choose the life you were born into, but where you start does not determine where you finish. Fix your thoughts on what is true, what is honorable, what is right, what is pure, lovely, and admirable. Think about things that are excellent and worthy of praise. "Finally, brethren, whatsoever things are true, whatsoever things are honest, whatsoever things are just, whatsoever things are pure, whatsoever things are lovely, whatsoever things are of good report; if there be any virtue, and if there be any praise, think on these things" (Phil. 4:8 NLT).

The key point in Philippians 4:13 lies in the words *through Christ*. Yes, of course you can do all things, but it's through Christ that you can. He (Christ) is the one who will give you strength to carry out the assignments you have before you. He is the one who will confirm whether the assignment is meant for you at all or if it is meant for someone else. And He will make all things come together easily for you to accomplish your assignment without losing sleep. Everything you think or plan to do should be through Him.

When you change your thinking, you change your life!

PART 2

She stood in the storm, and when the wind

did not blow her way, she adjusted her Sail.

—Elizabeth Edwards

CHAPTER 4

The Storm

Happenstance is a coincidental unplanned-for event. For example, if you call your brother on the phone, that's intentional. But if you bump into him in a restaurant, it's happenstance.

Vocabulary.com tells us that happenstance is a combination of the words *happen* and *circumstance*. Whereas circumstances are the conditions that surround an event, happenstance is the event itself. If you have no food at home and as a result go out to eat and sit next to a charming person who you end up marrying, your meeting was happenstance and you being hungry and having no food at home were the circumstances surrounding it.

Happenstance is what I choose to call what I experienced

on October 11, 2016. On this glorious day, I encountered an unbelievable scenario that amazed me beyond my comprehension.

I woke up and did my morning routine of worshipping and thanking God in prayer while still lying in bed. When I got out of bed, I noticed a tingling in my right thumb. I ignored it and kept shaking my hand, hoping it would stop. By the time I made it to the bathroom and back, I noticed my right leg and right hand felt a bit heavy. My husband asked me why I kept making a *hmmm* sound, the usual questioning sound one makes when he or she is unsure about something. I told him what I had noticed. He said, "Maybe the way you slept," and I concurred that it definitely must have been the way I slept.

My husband left the house to drop the boys off at school and called me on his way to tell me he had left his wallet at home and would be turning back to get it because his license was inside it.

Before he got back to the house, I got dressed so I could

go with them this time. Upon their return, I got into the car and left with them.

Later that morning, I was supposed to meet my study group at a coffee shop on the other side of town by 11:00 a.m.—the Starbucks on Main Street by the medical center.

So after dropping my husband at his office, I headed to my meeting. I drove myself there even though I still had those strange feelings in my hand and leg.

I got there earlier than the others, so I parallel parked, went in, secured a table big enough for all of us, and waited. But I noticed my right hand and leg felt even heavier than before. I kept praying for it to stop and telling myself that it must be because of my sleeping position the night before.

When the other ladies in my study group arrived, I told them about my symptoms. Later, when I got up to get breakfast, I had trouble pulling my debit card out of my wallet with my right hand, but I eventually won the struggle, as I refuse to give in. After a while, one of the ladies said she thought I needed some pain medicine, so we went across the street to a pharmaceutical store. When we entered the store, she suggested we talk to the pharmacist before picking a medicine off the shelf. We spoke to the pharmacist, and she advised me not to take aspirin.

She explained that aspirin might make what I was feeling worse. I asked how she was able to diagnose what I was feeling right there. She said that from my description of my symptoms, it sounded like I was having a stroke. I giggled and said, "No way!" She said since that was her diagnosis, giving me aspirin might cause more damage because if it was either a hemorrhagic stroke or an ischemic stroke, the aspirin would make it bleed more. She told me to head to the emergency room as soon as possible.

At this point, I decided to call my husband to come get me and the car. He came over, and we did as the pharmacist advised. We were closer to my doctor's office, but because I did not have an appointment with him for that day, my husband suggested we go to an emergency room that we'd been to before and that we knew to be less busy, which would allow me to get immediate attention. So, we went to the hospital closer to where I live.

Upon pulling up to the front entrance, I got out of the car by myself so my husband could go park the car. At this time, I could still walk, though my steps were heavier than before. I told the nurse at the reception desk what I was feeling and that I needed to see a doctor. She gave me a form to fill out, but I realized I couldn't write because my hand was now too weak to hold a pen. By this time, my husband came in, and I told him to sign the form.

Shortly after that, the nurse called me into an exam space and checked my vitals. Everything looked good, especially my blood pressure, which was 120 over 80. Next, she checked my temperature, and it was 96 which meant no fever. Then she asked me a series of questions:

Nurse: Do you smoke?

Me: No.

Nurse: Do you drink alcohol?

Me: No.

Nurse: Do you use drugs?

Me: No.

Then she said to wait for the doctor.

The doctor came in and said he had looked at my chart and that he would need to do a CT scan because my vitals gave no clue of what could have caused the stroke.

Surprisingly, the CT scan showed an old sign of distress on the blood vessels in my brain. The doctor asked me if I had ever had a severe injury to my head. I recalled the severe nonstop seven-day headache I had in the summer of 2014 that had landed me at the hospital. They had diagnosed it as a migraine. The doctor then said those marks couldn't have caused the stroke.

After I gave him the history of the headache, the doctor decided to keep me in the ER overnight for observation. Some of our family friends stopped by that night to check on me, and my pastor came by too. They all prayed with me for God's intervention. My husband later went home with my boys to sleep and get them ready for school the next day.

The next morning, the doctor came back to tell me that he still couldn't see anything that might have triggered or caused the stroke and that they would need to conduct an MRI. At this point, my right hand and leg were still affected

by the stroke, but my speech and face were not. After the MRI results came back clear, he said he had requested for a neurologist to examine me.

Later that afternoon, the neurologist came and did another CT scan and MRI and still found nothing. He then said he would have to do a more thorough examination of my brain, so he scheduled me for an angiogram the following day.

An angiogram is an X-ray test that uses a special dye and camera to take pictures of the blood flow in an artery or veins in the head, arms, legs, chest, back, or belly. During an angiogram, a thin tube called a catheter is placed into a blood vessel in the groin.

Can you hear me speaking like a medical student? I guess that's what staying longer in the hospital turns you into—a medical student.

That night, my pastor came back and prayed with me and anointed me as well. We all believed in the power of prayer, and we knew that God is able to correct everything. However, no one knows how and exactly when He will do what He decides to do. We are only certain that the end result will be better and more worth it than what we expect.

"Now all glory to God, who is able, through his mighty power at work within us, to accomplish infinitely more than we might ask or think" (Eph. 3:20 NLT).

The next morning, Thursday, October 13, 2016, I was taken to the theater room where the angiogram would be performed. The nurse prepped me, and the doctor came to talk to me. He advised me to stay still during the procedure, and I requested not to be given any sedative and that they only numb my groin on the right side, where they would be going in through. They did as I requested, and I remained conscious and alert all through the procedure. When they were done, they moved me into another room beside the theater, and I noticed the doctors and nurses looking at me strangely. The nurse began to ask me a series of questions like she had before we went in for the procedure.

First, she asked me, "What is your name?" I tried to answer, but it was difficult for me to talk, as my speech had become slurred. I heard the announcer saying, "Code blue," and noticed more doctors coming into the room. They were all looking at me in dismay. It took me almost three minutes to call out my husband's phone number when they asked so that they could call him to come downstairs to the theater from the waiting room.

Upon my husband's arrival, he saw me and exclaimed, "No! No!! No!!! Bukola, what happened?" I looked at him and stammered, "What is it?" He then explained that the right side of my face was drooping while the left was still okay. I couldn't speak well, and my right hand and leg couldn't move again.

Suddenly, I heard the doctors calling for the air flight crew. The neurologist came closer and said they had to transfer me to their downtown hospital at the medical center because it was a bigger facility and that more doctors needed to attend to me over there. Then the flight crew came and transported me downtown in a helicopter, but my husband was not allowed to ride with me.

When we arrived at the bigger hospital facility, doctors were waiting. As soon as we landed, they and some nurses came to wheel me in. They asked questions of the flight man as he briefed them about my case. I was alert and wondering if this was really happening to me or if I was in an episode of *Grey's Anatomy*.

The doctors started examining me and asked me a series of questions to confirm what was on the file the other doctors had sent them. The neurologist then told me that, based on what had occurred and her own evaluation, they'd need to do another angiogram. I was immediately wheeled to the theater.

They performed the angiogram, and I was transferred to the intensive care unit afterward. That same night, my immediate sister arrived and stayed with me in the ICU along with my husband, who had to spend most of the night in the waiting room because only one person was allowed to stay overnight with me.

By the next morning, I was told that the right side of my face had started to gradually move back to its original position, but I couldn't confirm it since I had no access to a mirror.

There is a man whose path God divinely orchestrated my path to cross. His name is Dr. William. Ever since we met, he had always looked out for me in his prayers. He can tell when I'm pretending or when I'm really good.

He had called me the previous Sunday morning, October 9, 2016, and said I'd been on his mind and that he and his wife had been praying for me, so he was calling to make sure I was okay and doing well, and I confirmed that I was. So Tuesday, after I was diagnosed with a minor stroke, I called him to let him know where I was, and he started praying for me and raised a prayer alter with his prayer team.

When he called on Thursday to check on me, he couldn't reach me, but he spoke to my husband. He kept calling and monitoring my progress. Then he drove down to see me the next night. He, my sister, my husband, and I prayed and had communion.

However, something strange happened while he was in my room praying. The heartbeat and blood pressure monitor that was attached to my chest blanked out. When we were done, the nurse came in and asked why we had switched it off. We said none of us touched it. She was surprised and said maybe the cord twisted.

Later that night, the doctors told me that so far all they could say was that the stroke had been caused by acute stress and that while I was here in the hospital, they needed to put me on strict monitoring. That meant no cell phones and no guests until further notice. Just sleep and rest.

Four days later, I was moved out of the ICU and into the stroke unit.

The doctors were still doing a lot of research and testing on me to find out what could have caused the stroke. They took blood samples almost every two hours. At this time, I had stabilized a lot and was allowed to have limited guests during the day.

On Sunday, October 16, 2016, my pastor visited me, along with a team of ministers from church, and they prayed with me, my husband, and my sister.

On Monday morning, the doctors told me they had to do another procedure called a lumbar puncture. A lumbar puncture is a procedure to collect and look at the fluid surrounding the brain and spinal cord. It is usually done by carefully inserting a needle into the low spinal canal to draw the fluid. The procedure was successfully carried out that same day. While they waited for the results of different types of blood tests, CT scans, and MRIs, the neurologist cared so much about me and wanted to help me in every way possible. She immediately ordered therapy to start, and the oral therapy and physical therapy began the same day. She signed me up for rehab within the hospital building. Later that day, I was moved from the stroke unit to another ward in the hospital called the neuroscience acute care.

All sorts of tests were carried out daily in an effort to determine what could have triggered my stroke.

During the week, when Dr. William called to check up on me, the monitors in my room went off again while he was praying with me over the phone.

Professor Oscar stopped at the hospital to pray with me and also encouraged me to not lose my focus on God and to remain strong through it all. Professor Oscar said, "If medicine can't identify what is going on with you, then you and I know it's spiritual, which can only be dealt with spiritually." He said the doctors were simply fishing for other things that might have caused the stroke. He had communion with my husband and me before leaving.

On Monday afternoon, October 24, 2016, the doctors came into my room and told me that my platelet count had been dropping for some days now and that they had been monitoring it, hoping it would get better with time and medication changes, but it had dropped too far and too drastically. I asked them how low.

The doctor said I had come in with a count of 165 and it had dropped to 97 and then to 36 and now to 17. They checked all over my body to make sure I wasn't bleeding anywhere and warned me to be very careful so that I didn't cut or bruise myself because if that happened, they wouldn't be able to stop the bleeding.

The neurologist came in to tell me that I wouldn't be able to continue with the rehab exercises because of the platelet count so as to avoid any accident or injury. Then they moved me back to the stroke unit and hooked the monitor back up to my chest.

By the following morning, it had dropped again—this time to 9—and they had no other choice than to infuse me with platelets. They did one pint of platelets that day, and by the next day, my count had dropped again. This time they rushed two bags of platelets and kept watching to see if my count would drop off again. I prayed for it, and my family joined me in prayer concerning the platelets.

That evening, I was told that I didn't need another platelet infusion because the trend had changed from dropping to going up and that the last time they checked, my count had moved up from 7 to 12. By the time I went to bed that night, it had risen to 19. All the doctors let out sighs of relief about the upward trend of my platelets.

On Wednesday, I woke up around 4:00 a.m., and Pastor Creflo Dollar was on TBN, which is the only channel I was watching in my room. He said, "As a believer, whatever you believe will be tested." Those words struck a chord in me and kept ringing in my ears.

He went on to say that the test comes in every form you can imagine, including your finances, your children, your marriage, your health, and your ministry. The tests are to see if truly you belong to Jesus as you profess or if you'll give up under pressure.

About an hour later, my nurse for the day walked into my room with a bag of blood in his hand and my morning medicines.

I asked him, "Please, who and what is the blood for?"

He replied, "It's for you, ma'am."

I laughed, sarcastically touching my chest, and said, "Me?"

He said yes, and I responded, "No way."

Then I asked him exactly why I would need a blood infusion, and he said it was because when they checked my vitals that morning, the tests had shown that while my platelet count was slowly rising, my hemoglobin had dropped. Then I asked how far it had dropped. He said to 6.9. I asked what number it was at before, and he said it had dropped from 7 to 6.9. Then I asked him why I was

just hearing about my hemoglobin dropping now. He kept quiet. Instantly I became angry in my spirit. I told the nurse I was not taking that blood, and the nurse said the doctor had instructed them to infuse me with blood once my hemoglobin dropped below 7.

I told him to page the doctor and let him know that I said I was not taking any blood. So he left my room and said he would have to return the bag of blood to the blood bank. I shrugged like I was saying *whatever*.

When he left my room, I looked up at the ceiling and told myself, *Bukola, this is war!*

I had come here with a stroke, and they had bypassed that. Now all sorts of blood issues were showing up, from my platelet count dropping without any cuts, clots, or bruises to my hemoglobin levels now dropping. This had to stop, and I had to leave now.

I remembered what I had heard from the pastor on the TV earlier that morning. He'd said that whatever I believed would be tested. I realized that this was a test of my faith in

God, whose I am and in whom I believe. I also remembered the words of Professor Oscar; he'd said this was spiritual.

Everything that was happening had no medical explanation again. The doctors kept assuming it was the medicines they were giving me. For instance, when I asked why my platelet and hemoglobin counts had gone down, they said they suspected it was the heparin. (Heparin is an anticoagulant, or blood thinner, which prevents the formation of blood clots. Heparin is used to treat and prevent blood clots in the veins, arteries, or lungs.)

I went ahead and prayed, asking God to arise on my behalf, show me mercy, and grant me victory. I broke bread (took communion) with the crackers and apple juice in my room and started praising God for the victory. When my husband came in that morning after dropping the boys off at school, I told him what had transpired, and he agreed with me in prayer again, together we asked for my hemoglobin count to go up without any blood transfusion.

The doctor came to my room during his rounds, and I confirmed that I had told the nurse not to infuse me with the blood. I then requested if I could have the test again.

He agreed to redo the test but said I would have to wait few hours because it had to be done in six-hour intervals. So the nurse came in later to draw blood to send to the lab.

I turned on my iPad and started praising God for what He had done, what He was doing, and what He would do.

At noon, the nurse came in to draw blood samples again. I kept waiting for the results, but nothing came and I couldn't press the bell beside me because I didn't have any emergency needs.

The nurse came back to my room around 2:00 p.m. to give me my afternoon medicines, and I asked him if the test results were out. He said they were and that it was good now. I asked why I hadn't gotten the results on time, and he said, "It's good news if you don't get a call back from the hospital after a test. No news is good news." My hemoglobin count had moved from 6.9 to 8.2. I sighed in relief. That was how I overcame all the blood issues.

A doctor from the building's rehabilitation center came to examine me and said I was responding well and recovering faster than expected. Shortly after, the neurologist came in and examined me as well. Then she made a joke that I must be faking it because my grip was much stronger than prior days. I told her I was not. We both laughed at that, and she said she was just so surprised at how fast I was regaining strength on my right side. I was so moved by her act of kindness and compassion. She kept saying, "You are too young and too full of life for a stroke."

I explained to her that all the progress she was seeing had nothing to do with me; I was as amazed as she was, if not more.

The next day, Friday, at 8:00 p.m., I was discharged from the hospital to the glory of the Lord. However, I was reluctant to leave because I was worried about how to take care of myself and help my children because I had been assisted with everything at the hospital and still had some weakness on my right side. I was sent home walking with a cane.

I am still in awe of how God works. It was just because of His love and mercy, not because of anything I have done or have not done, just His unfailing *love*.

Rise above the Storm,

And you will find the Sunshine.

—Mario Fernandez

Rise above the Storm,

And you will find the Sunshine.

—Mario Fernandez

CHAPTER 5

After the Storm

Storms are in our lives to stir stuff up. Yet it is from the peaceful aftermath that we gain insight.

After the life-changing storm in your life—the one that you never saw coming, something you weren't prepared for, something that you couldn't make sense of, something that beats the human norm and makes everyone question if it was ever real—what do you do?

Yes, what do you do?

For me, I got up and thanked God for another lease on life, a fresh start, renewed vigor, and good health. Suddenly, life had new meaning to me. The Billy Ocean lyrics "There's beauty up above and things we never take notice of" became so true for me.

I felt so amazed about what I had just come through. It was too rapid and shocking. I couldn't make sense of it at all. I spent my days and nights asking myself if it was real, how it happened, and how I came out of it. All these questions ran through my head, but amid it all, I was so grateful and in awe of how God had restored me. The storm had come on so fast and tempestuously, but God reversed it more quickly than it started.

Then the phase I never saw coming hit me from out of nowhere. The unimaginable questions and assumptions I encountered, the critics, the notion that I owed anyone an explanation, and the judgments increased daily.

I had to stay away from the crowd because the news about my stroke was shocking to so many, and a lot of people had many questions for my husband and I. So we decided it was pointless receiving guests at home because it would interrupt my rest time and ongoing therapy.

Nonetheless, whenever and wherever we ran into someone, they asked all sorts of question: How did it happen? When did it happen? What was she doing?

Then I encounter some "Christianys" (overly extreme Christians) With Christianys, nothing you say or do says you are righteous unless it is done according to their standard. They seldom talk to you, and when they do, they do so indirectly so you probably won't be able to say they are directly talking to you.

Some of their statements to me went like this: We all need to move closer to God because if we are closer to God, we can't be sick. We need to take our Christianity serious ... etc.

I just smiled and kept quiet. But in my mind, I really wanted to ask them what the yardstick was for measuring how strong our Christian walks are? Is there a Bible study log that one needs to sign every day? Or if the scripture is not the first thing that flies out every time someone opens his or her mouth, does that make his or her Christianity unreal? Or if someone has been tried by hardship over and over again, does that make that person a weak, unbelieving Christian?

But since I'm not Christ and am just a human trying

to walk in His ways as I best understand them and work on things that easily beset me and lead to stress, I ignored most of their comments.

I had to actually respond one day when someone walked up to my husband and I and said what happened to me was because of my service to the church, especially in my assignment in the protocol team and assisting with my pastor's meetings.

My service within the church, working with the pastor, and serving on the protocol team had nothing to do with me having a stroke. Some of the members of my stroke support group were not Christians, had never served in any capacity, and still had strokes.

As a believer in the Lord Jesus Christ, the day, hour, and minute you made the decision to follow Christ and make Him your Lord and Savior, you became an enemy of Satan and entered into spiritual warfare. There are different types of spiritual warfare, including the battle of the mind, discouragement, and laziness to study the word. Satan will distract you with things of this world, especially the things he knows you love. The enemy won't lure you with what you don't like; he knows he can't get you that way. To catch a monkey, you bait the trap with bananas.

The enemy has only one assignment for believers: "the thief's purpose is to steal, kill and destroy" (John 10:10 NLT).

However, at same time you gave your life to Christ, you got a special covering. You then need to activate that covering by studying the word of God and living in the assurance that you are His child and He's got your back. "The Lord is my light and my salvation so why should I be afraid? The Lord is my fortress, protecting me from danger, so why should I tremble? When evil people come to devour me, when my enemies and foes attack me, they will stumble and fall" (Ps. 27:1–2 NLT).

So as a believer, whether you choose to serve in the house of God (church) or not, as long as you are saved by Christ, they will come; you might not see them as attacks, but we all go through them at various levels and times.

Nehemiah's building of the wall wasn't preaching the

gospel, but it was something that everybody eventually realized was accomplished by God (Neh. 6:16 NLT) It was a work of the Lord. In the same way, when we are doing the work of the Lord, wherever He has called us, we are working for him and, therefore, will incur the attacks of the enemy in various forms.

I have served in various departments since my walk with Christ began, but the most fulfilling assignment I've ever had was to serve as a protocol officer.

Some have called me the pastor's maid or servant, but I see it as Aaron and Hur in Exodus 17:11–12: "As long as Moses held up his hands, the Israelites were winning, but whenever he lowered his hands, the Amalekites were winning. Moses' arms soon became so tired he could no longer hold them up. So, Aaron and Hur found a stone for him to sit on. Then they stood on each side of Moses, holding up his hands. So, his hands held steady until sunset" (NLT).

Pastors are humans like you and me; they just have a title. They live here on earth, go through same things we do (or more), have the same president, spend the same currency, and are afflicted in same ways (or even more). If all I am called to do is find a way to lighten the load they carry, which hopefully will allow them to spend more time in God's presence to bring the word to the needy that day, I feel a sense of accomplishment.

Serving God by doing activities in church for the success of the service does not equate Christ's love. You can work tirelessly in the house of God and still live a defeated life. Your knowing Christ and having a personal relationship with Him is the ultimate.

God did send my husband and I a lot of people who stood by us through the storm. Some fasted and prayed constantly, 24-7, even though they didn't have access to us at the hospital. Our pastor and his family filled the gap. We have uncles who raised prayer teams on the mission ground and friends who became our family by taking my kids into their homes and making sure they didn't miss a single day of school and who kept their minds at peace so their grades didn't drop in school. Some blessed us monetarily and fellowshipped with us to stabilize our livelihood. All of this help and assistance were things I see as sent by God. I appreciate each and every person who supported us, but ultimate glory goes to Christ alone.

Life here on earth is both a testing ground and a battleground. Our faith, what we profess and believe, will be tested at various times throughout our lifetime. Likewise, we will have to fight for what is rightfully given to us in Christ Jesus. He paid the price for it already, so we must not allow the enemy to toil with what is ours by right. As parents, we won't allow anyone mess with our children; we ought to guide and protect our victory in Christ in the same way. We should value and cherish what Christ has given us. No one else has even given his only son just to save you. We must always keep in mind our pledge of fidelity to be good soldiers under our captain.

> We are human but we don't wage war as
> humans do, we use God's mighty weapons,
> not worldly weapons, to knock down the

strongholds of human reasoning and to destroy false arguments, we destroy every proud obstacle that keeps people from knowing God. We capture their rebellious thoughts and teach them to obey Christ. (2 Cor. 10:3–5 NLT)

Do not resist or run from difficulties in your life. These problems are not random mistakes; they are hand-tailored blessings designed for your benefit and growth. Embrace all the circumstances in your life, trusting God to bring good out of them. View problems as opportunities to rely more fully on God. When you start to feel stressed, let those feelings alert you to your need of God. Thus, your needs act an entryway into a deep dependence on God and increasing intimacy with Him.

God's path to pure joy is spelled out in the book of James:

Dear brothers and sisters, "when troubles come your way, consider it an opportunity for great joy, for you know that when your faith is tested, your endurance has a chance to grow, so let it grow, for when your endurance is fully developed, you will be perfect and complete, needing nothing. (1:2–4 NLT)

The Christian life is one of persistence—sticking to our tasks and not giving up. That is the admonition of Ephesians 6:18: "Pray in the spirit at all times and on every occasion. Stay alerted and be persistent in your prayers for all believers everywhere" (NLT). And in Luke 10:19: "I have given you authority to trample on snakes and scorpions and to overcome all the power of the enemy; nothing will harm you" (NIV). And also in Isaiah 54:17: "No weapon formed against you shall prosper, and every tongue which rises against you in judgment, you shall condemn. This is the heritage of the servants of the Lord, and their righteousness is of me, says the Lord" (KJV).

This scripture didn't say that as a believer you won't be attacked; it didn't say the weapon won't form. It simply means that the weapons will form, but they won't just prosper!

As believers in Jesus Christ, our faith does not affirm that all things we go through in life will be good; neither does it mean if you don't have faith, all things will be bad.

Satan has his ways. He wants us to lose faith in God when things are not working out as we have planned and hoped.

When you think having maximum faith in God means nothing evil will happen to you, that belief is wrong.

Complete faith in God is knowing that God already has a better plan for us, much better than we can even imagine, and acknowledging Him in everything we do. Faith in Him is absolute confidence that He is more than able to deliver us from all troubles, even those that challenge our faith. It is important that we understand that God is more than able to deliver us and calm any storm we may encounter. Anything less than this assurance diminishes our faith and will not allow us to grow in Him.

It is the things we are unsure of that require a greater level of trust. But with God, whatever you consider a risk in trusting Him is worth it. The more you spend time with Him, the more He reveals Himself to you and the easier it will be for you to trust Him. He doesn't always allow us to know the exact time that things in His plan will be fulfilled, but trusting in His timing will put our minds at peace.

"I have told you all this so that you may have peace in me. Here on earth, you will have many trials and sorrows. But take heart, because I have overcome the world" (John 16:33 NLT).

"For I hold you by your right hand—I, am the Lord your God. And I say to you, don't be afraid. I am here to help you" (Isa. 41:13 NLT).

Always remember, when God fights your battle, victory is the only outcome.

PART 3

You cannot escape the responsibility of tomorrow by evading it today.

—Abraham Lincoln

CHAPTER 6

Expect Responsibility

With every gift comes demand, and with every blessing comes responsibility. When we receive God's blessings, we must use them wisely and responsibly.

Owing a home is an incredible blessing, something that a lot of us unfortunately take for granted. The blessing of home ownership, however, also comes with a tremendous amount of responsibility. There are monthly payments, occasional repairs to make, regular cleaning to be done, yards to keep up, and from time to time, improvements to make.

In the end, you cannot enjoy the blessing of home ownership unless you are willing to take on the responsibilities that come with it.

When you receive a miracle, there is a charge, or responsibility, attached to it. This shown in the Bible when Jesus healed the leper in Luke 5:12–15:

> While Jesus was in one of the towns, a man came along who was covered with leprosy. When he saw Jesus, he fell with his face to the ground and begged him, "Lord, if you are willing, you can make me clean." Jesus reached out his hand and touched the man. "I am willing," he said. "Be clean!" And immediately the leprosy left him. *Then Jesus ordered him, "Don't tell anyone, but go, show yourself to the priest and offer the sacrifices that Moses commanded for your cleansing, as a testimony to them."* Yet the news about him spread all the more, so that crowds of people came to hear him and to be healed of their sicknesses. (NIV, emphasis mine)

It is also shown when he healed the two blind men in Mark 8:22–26:

> They came to Bethsaida, and some people brought a blind man and begged Jesus to touch him. He took the blind man by the hand and led him outside the village. When he had spit on the man's eyes and put his hands on him, Jesus asked, "Do you see anything?" He looked up and said, "I see people; they look like trees walking around." Once more Jesus put his hands on the man's eyes. Then his eyes were opened, his sight was restored, and he saw everything clearly. *Jesus sent him home, saying, "Don't even go into the village."* (NIV, emphasis mine)

Another example is when He fed five thousand men and their families:

Jesus said, "Have the people sit down." There was plenty of grass in that place, and they sat down (about five thousand men were there). Jesus then took the loaves, gave thanks, and distributed to those who were seated as much as they wanted. He did the same with the fish. When they had all had enough to eat, he said to his disciples, *"Gather the pieces that are left over. Let nothing be wasted."* So, they gathered them and filled twelve baskets with the pieces of the five barley loaves left over by those who had eaten. (John 6:10–12 NIV, emphasis mine)

After Jesus left the region of Tyre, some people brought to him a man who was deaf and had difficulty speaking. Jesus miraculously healed the man of both ailments. As explained in the gospel of Mark 7:31–37:

Then Jesus left the vicinity of Tyre and went through Sidon, down to the Sea of Galilee and into the region of the Decapolis. There some people brought to him a man who was deaf and could hardly talk, and they begged Jesus to place his hand on him.

After he took him aside, away from the crowd, Jesus put his fingers into the man's ears. Then he spits and touched the man's tongue. He looked up to heaven and with a deep sigh said to him, "Ephphatha!" (which means "Be opened!"). At this, the man's ears were opened, his tongue was loosened and he began to speak plainly. *Jesus commanded them not to tell anyone.* But the more he did so, the more they kept talking about it. People were overwhelmed with amazement. "He has done everything well," they said.

"He even makes the deaf hear and the mute
speak." (NIV, emphasis mine)

In all of these passages, we see that there's a charge, some
sort of responsibility given after they received the miracle
from Christ, and each responsibility was different. It is up
to you to discover what the Lord is asking you to do after
you come out of the storm.

I believe one of the utmost things to do after seeing
God move miraculously in our circumstances is to testify
of His goodness, to let the whole world know and come to
the knowledge of our God and the wonders of His power
and love. The method or means by which you get the word
out should be according to His direction.

He delivered me from a stroke and restored me back to
the way He created me, but I wasn't released to shout out the
experience as I would have loved to, until now. Even though,
I shared it with my family and a few friends, I couldn't go
into all the details publicly. Hence, the reason for this book
at this appointed time.

If it's worth doing at all

It's worth doing well

---McGraw-Hill Dictionary of American

Idioms and phrasal verbs

CHAPTER 7

All In

Oftentimes, as Christians we think our secular life is different from our spiritual life. But it's not. If you love Christ, you will live for Him in every area of your life—your home, marriage, school, career, finances, children, health, etc. You accepted Him and invited Him; you might as well go all the way. The moment you give your life to Christ, you have entered into a lifelong relationship with Him in every aspect of your life and there is no separation from your Christ life and secular life. We gradually fall into the separation unconsciously when we start seeing some situations as things that we can handle.

We fondly and casually say, "I've got this." Yeah, you've

got it, but ask yourself this: Is the way you've always done it, or is it the way Christ wants you to do it this time around?

There is nothing we know how to do excellently that's not given by God.

I was living with the delusion that I could do this, I could do that, and I had done it, mastered it, and gotten recognitions for it, but was that the way Christ wanted those things done? Were they done with appreciation toward God. He is the one who has given you and me the ability to do something and perfect it, and we should consult him every time.

No matter how successful you have become doing the same thing repeatedly, you are still to reach out to him. "Whatever is good and perfect is a gift coming down to us from God our Father, who created all the lights in the heavens. He never changes or casts a shifting shadow" (James 1:17 NLT).

So that talent you have is a gift from God, and because we know He never changes, we can trust Him to keep improving it, making it better and better, if only we recognize that. The same God who gave you those gifts—like cleaning, organizing, arranging, administration, speaking, writing, talking, beautifying, color coordination, styling, etc.—never changes. Let go and let God!

Motive is crucial in everything we do. Have you ever had someone do something nice for you or act nicely toward you and then you later found out that he or she was doing it to manipulate you into doing something for him or her? The ulterior motive canceled out everything nice that that person did. Your motive for giving yourself totally to God is crucial. Some dedicate themselves to God to work out their guilt. For others, like me, it's because of His love, mercy, and grace toward me.

I made a covenant with God when I was diagnosed with the weak immune disease, and I vowed that as long as He keeps me alive, I shall serve Him with all my heart and might.

This has been the driving force that keeps me going. Even when I am tired, I kept going on. Unknown to so many people who called me names and judged me, I've had to deal with some difficult guests, ministers, and church members in my line of duty. Some will push you to the wall, but I have chosen to walk through the wall rather than turn back and give them a piece of my mind. I think some of the people who were just determined to make me fall got a taste of it, but in all, I thank God for His mercy. His mercy refuses to let me die, and His love took my place.

"Endure suffering along with me, as a good soldier of Christ" (2 Tim. 2:3 NLT).

My service unto Him doesn't make Him love me more than others; neither does it make Him answer me every time I call upon Him. He just loves me with all my faults and without judging me. He loves me!

Life is a series of problems. Either you are in one now, you're just coming out of one, or you're getting ready to go into one. No matter how good things are in your life, there is always something bad that needs to be worked on, and no matter how bad things are in your life, there is always something good for which you can thank God.

Christ is love. His nature is love. There is nothing you

can do to change that. He will still be faithful to you even when you are unfaithful to Him. "If we are unfaithful, He remains faithful, for he cannot deny who he is" (2 Tim. 2:13 NLT). He is good to you because that's just the way He is and not because of what you do or what you've done. It wasn't His birth that changed our life but His death. God responds to faith. Our faith in Him, not our need, moves Him. Our faith is what causes Him to act on our behalf. We'll never be able to develop that kind of faith, that kind of trust and confidence, in Him if we don't spend enough time with Him to get to know Him.

Have confidence in God. Hold on to a strong faith, the kind of faith that is backed up with a complete knowledge and understanding that with God's help you can do anything and overcome all. Replace your fears with faith and then watch what God will do.

No matter how great we become in life, we cannot be greater than God, and Jesus Christ has paid the price for us all. No man has ever died and risen again after three days.

If you know of any, let me know. And I mean dead, not in a coma.

John 15:5 says, "Yes, I am the vine; you are the branches. Those who remain in me, and I in them, will produce much fruit. For apart from me you can do nothing" (NLT).

And Ephesians 2:8–10 reads,

> God saved you by his grace when you believed. And you can't take credit for this; it is a gift from God. Salvation is not a reward for the good things we have done, so none of us can boast about it. For we are God's masterpiece. He has created us anew in Christ Jesus, so we can do the good things he planned for us long ago. (NLT)

God is in control of everything, and when we commit all to Him, we will triumph.

He assures peace. He told us not to be afraid, for He is with us. No matter what happens, He will never leave you or forsake you. Let this assurance soak into your heart and mind until you overflow with joy.

The media relentlessly proclaim bad news. A daily diet of their fare will sicken you. Instead of focusing on their news, tune into the living word, which is always same and comforting.

In Deuteronomy 31:6 NLT, it says, "To be strong and courageous! Do not be afraid and do not panic before them. For the Lord, your God will personally go ahead of you. He will neither fail you nor abandon you"

We live in a time when the most we are called to give God is a few hours a week and maybe a couple more on Sundays. We say, "Here, God, take this part of me, but I'm going to keep the rest." We compromise. Giving God everything isn't even on the radar. Social media, sports, and friendships fill up our time and deplete our physical energy when it should be devoted to God. It's not that sports, friends, and social media are bad in and of themselves, but when we put them before God, it becomes idolatry. "When we build our lives on anything else but God, that thing—though a good thing—becomes an enslaving addiction, something we have to have in order to be happy," says pastor and author Timothy Keller.[3] God cannot use people who are only partially devoted to Him. Jesus Christ changed the world with twelve men who were willing to give everything they had—including their lives—to His purpose and plan. Guillermo Maldonado says in his book *How to Walk in the Supernatural Power of God*, "The only ability God requires is availability. I don't know about you, but I want to stand before Christ one day and have Him say, "Well done, good and faithful servant" Matt 25:21 NLT

God wants our everything. He doesn't just want the good things in our lives but also the ugly and bad things. God loves as we are, but He does not leave us there. God's transforming power will change us if we let it because God does not just want everything; he will also give us everything.

Trust God from the bottom of your heart. Don't try to figure everything out on your own. Listen for God's voice

---

[3]   Dr. Timothy Keller, *The Reason for God*.

in everything you do and everywhere you go; He's the one who will keep you on track. Don't assume that you know it all.

Mary Demuth writes in her book *Everything*: "He [Jesus] wants all of us, all the time, our minds and hearts deeply engaged with His so we will joyfully follow Him toward every single adventure He plans for us. This is not me vowing to be a good girl or me planning to be holy. This is me (and you) daring to follow the leading of the Holy Spirit of God."[4] This is not about us forcing this to happen. This is not about us making this happen. This is about us letting God's grace do His work in us. This is about us daring to trust God and only God.

When we give something to God, it feels wonderful because we are essentially giving our burdens, worries, and cares about that thing over to Him. We are doing what Philippians 4:6 NLT instructs us to do, which is to, "Not to be anxious about anything, but in everything, by prayer

---

[4]   Mary Demuth, *Everything: what you give and what you gain to become like Jesus* (Thomas Nelson, 2012).

and petition, with thanksgiving, present your requests to God." And when we do this (present our requests to Him), we feel an overwhelming peace knowing that it is in His hands, which is what the next verse in Philippians chapter 4 explains will happen: "And the peace of God, which transcends all understanding, will guard your hearts and your minds in Christ Jesus."

However, a problem arises when we "take back" the thing we gave to Him. Whether it be taking back control of something we surrendered to Him, trying to take care of ourselves in an area of life, or trying to figure out our own way when we initially asked for His direction, all of these things will cause us to take back the very thing that we gave to God.

If you don't feel like you have ever had a true revelation of His great love for you, that is certainly the first step in trusting Him. All you have to do is simply ask the Lord to reveal His great love for you. I can promise that He wants to show you even more than you want Him to.

Also, you have to know His promises to you. Take the

area of finances, for example. If you don't know that He promised to provide all of your needs (Phil. 4:19 NLT) then you will never know that is something He told you that He would do, so you won't really know if you can hand that over to Him and trust Him with it. Knowing that He cares and that He has promised to take care of you will keep you calm.

God will sustain us. He will never let us fall. He cares for us.

God declares both His ability and His willingness to be our strength and support—mentally, emotionally, and spiritually. He is able and, best of all, willing to take everything that threatens to overwhelm us and use it for our benefit. He has promised to "work all things together for the good of those who love him, who have been called according to his purpose" Rom 8:28 Even during times when we doubt Him, He is still working for our good and His glory. And He has also promised that He will allow no trial to be so great that we cannot bear it and that He will provide a means of escape (1 Cor.10:13 NLT).

The temptations in your life are no different from what others experience. And God is faithful. He will not allow the temptation to be more than you can stand. When you are tempted, He will show you a way out so that you can endure.

By this He means that He will not let us fall, as He promised in Psalm 55:22: "Cast thy burden upon the LORD, and he shall sustain thee: he shall never suffer the righteous to be moved" (KJV).

When you truly give it all to the Lord, He is able to pour the elixir of His love, with all its healing power, into your heart in full measure. He can soothe, He can mend, He can heal any hurt, any pain, any past, and He will. Let's stop giving God what is left and start giving Him what is right! Give *all*!

PART 4

Sometimes you don't realize you're actually

drowning when you're trying to be everyone

else's anchor

--Daily Inspirational Quotes

CHAPTER 8

Pursuit of Me

After my stroke experience, I began to see things differently as I started to reevaluate my life and purpose here on earth. I had so many relationships going on simultaneously in my life: I had relationships with my husband, my sons, my business, my career, my family, my ministry, my friends, my fellowship, my acquaintances, etc., but none with myself.

Your relationship with yourself is the most valuable relationship you can have. This relationship sets the tone for every other relationship you have. I don't know how to explain the burden I had within me to take care of everyone.

As far back as I could remember, I just wanted to make sure everyone I came into contact with was doing well. Whether I was asked for assistance or not, I made it my duty to care for them. Sometimes it was apparent that they did not need anything, but after spending few hours with them, I would discover something I could care for in them.

Some people have said to me that it's a good thing to care for others. Other people have said I'm so caring because I need something from them. Contrary to those assumptions, I feel fulfilled when I am able to do things for other.

I can visit you and just be in your kitchen cleaning up or arranging stuff without being asked to. I guess maybe another reason why I care so much is because I can't stand seeing people helpless or confused.

Someone simply by saying, "I don't know how," around me automatically makes it my business to start thinking of how to, even when I'm not sure how to either.

As women, we always want to please people, especially our families, but we need to take a stand against getting out of balance in this area. You must take care of yourself in order to take care of anyone else. I heard this saying from Iyanla Vanzant on *The Oprah Winfrey Show*. She said: "You can only give from the left over; when you are full, whatever spills over is what you are supposed to give." Psalm 23:5(b) says, "My cup runs over." 5NLT, it only runs over after it's full.

Just ask God to help you to know when to pull back and restore yourself while taking care of others.

The stroke served as a warning sign for me to take things easy and make taking care of me priority. I started looking at my life from a new perspective. When I was told the stroke had been stress induced and I searched my life, I couldn't find anything tangible that I considered stressful. Everything I was engaged in was what an average married woman did, but I discovered I had made it my responsibility to look after my husband and boys. I became aware of how much I looked out for them and how much I wanted to fix everything. When things were not going well in our house, when we had issues, I made it my responsibility to find a way to solve it.

I would pray about it, fast about it, read about it, and then start investigating and strategizing how to fix it now right now. I would get so worked up that I would start fighting with my husband, who simply prayed about it and let it go.

When I asked him why he didn't care about how to fix things as much as I did, he said there was not point worrying about how to fix something you have prayed about and that if you knew how to fix it, you probably wouldn't pray about it. I learned a lesson from that, which I recommend you practice.

You should never worry about whatever you commit to God. The fact that you trusted Him to handle it was why you reached out to Him in the first place. Worrying exalts the devil, who is the author of fear; at the same time, it diminishes God in your situation. God, who is the author of faith. Whatever you exalt is your god—fear or faith.

Worrying about how, when, and what is fear, and it can be very stressful once it consumes you.

How you treat yourself is how you treat God. If you put yourself last, you put God last. You are the representation of God on earth, so putting other things above yourself means you are putting those things above God. In your life, you've got to be as good to yourself as you want to be to God in order to be of service to others in the world. It's not selfish to put yourself first; it's self-full. What is inside the cup is for you, and what runs out of it is for others. So you always have to keep your cup full in order to give to others. These does not mean that you disregard them. It means that you need to be whole to reach others; otherwise, you both will end up drained.

We often think that giving so much and inconveniencing ourselves earns us a special seat in heaven. Sorry, but no, it doesn't. You only make the receiver a thief for taking from you everything you inconvenience yourself to give without them knowing that they are inconveniencing you. Soon you will begin to run away from those people and see them as opportunists or users. Meanwhile, they didn't ask you for it; you just put it on yourself to be God in their lives.

I used to think that as long as a person is saying he or she has a need for this or couldn't get something or uses phrases like, "I wish I had this" and so on, that individual is automatically wanting me to provide it. But I discovered the fallacy of that belief one day when a friend told another friend that she was tired of helping me and giving me stuff. I felt so mad because I had never asked this lady for anything; she had just stepped up to give me stuff, and I had thought it was just her way of expressing love.

If I talk about a need or something I want to do and can't do right now or simply compliment what you have on doesn't mean that I want it or that I want you to go get it for me. I have aunties I mess with like that, and they know if I want it, I'll just ask for it directly, no games of hide-and-seek. Just because someone is talking about what he or she is going through doesn't mean that person wants you to fix it. Maybe that person just feels comfortable talking with you about the thing that's troubling him or her, which means that he or she trusts you, not that he or she wants you to fix it.

Oftentimes, the person just needs a word of encouragement or for you to share a tough season that you've experienced, and that will give him or her a hopeful assurance. You may need to give your time and effort to really help in the matter or just pray with him or her. That is all that person needs, not money.

A lot of us Christians misinterpret the scripture in Proverbs 3:27: "do not withhold good from those who deserve it when it's in your power to help them" (NLT).

One of the key phrases here is "in your power." What is in your power is what you are expected to give, not what you will give and then go bankrupt afterward. What you have in your power might not be enough for you or for the other person you want to give to at the moment. Hence, we must always pray about what we are to give. Giving inconveniently and grudgingly does not glorify God. "You must each decide in your heart how much to give. And don't give reluctantly or in response to pressure. For God loves a person who gives cheerfully" (2 Cor. 9:7 NLT).

There are some fundamental actions I consider valuable in my attempt to love and pursue what is beneficial to me. Two follows here, and two more appear in the next chapter.

Accept It

In taking care of yourself, you will need to accept whatever situation you are facing. When you argue against reality, you will suffer. When you push against what is and want it to be different, you want the situation to be what it isn't. That is stress.

Accepting reality is not the same thing as liking it. You don't have to like the situation you are in, but you have to accept it to be able to change it. Don't feel guilty about whatever position in which you find yourself. Yes, as human beings, we look inward for the role we have played in what happened and how we've caused it, but dwelling on those thoughts makes it worse and stresses you out. Suppressing your feelings and ignoring the problem will never work well for you in the long term, and you know this. You should look for a healthy coping mechanism. For me, it's singing and dancing and then going on a prayer walk where I just talk to God.

For the sake of acceptance, write down why you can't change what is or the reasons you may be happy in the future that this happened. You aren't trying to eliminate the "bad" parts of you. You're trying to understand yourself and how you work. The side effect of that is that you will be a more efficient and enlightened you. Don't spend all your energy on fighting the old rather than building the new.

The situation you're in is what it is. No matter how much you wish for something different or reject it (and reject yourself), nothing will change it. However, by confronting your situation, you can at least begin to address it.

No one ever got a different result by doing the same thing repeatedly. In fact, expecting a different result from same action is one of the definitions of insanity. The way to heal faster and move beyond the pain is to accept it and find ways to nurture the wound. By accepting the present and analyzing how you got there and how to prevent it from repeating itself, you can overcome the pain as you create a happier, more fulfilling future.

When you complain and fight reality, you will lose every time. Once you accept the situation for what it truly is, not what you want it to be, you are free to move forward.

A situation that seems nasty, painful, and evil can become a source of beauty, joy, and strength if faced with an open mind.

Love You

Appreciate your life. When you appreciate, you have more appreciation equals multiplication. Know and understand that you are an excellent human being, created in the image of God. "So, God created human beings in his own image; In the image of God He created them; Male and female He created them" (Gen. 1:27 NLT). "Thank you for making me so wonderfully complex! Your workmanship is marvelous—how well I know it" (Ps. 139:14 NLT).

God created us uniquely. His purpose is not for us to have all things in common. Rather, His desire was for us to be diverse with one thing in common—*Him*!

Take a look at what Paul wrote to the Philippians in the Bible in Philippians 4:19: "And this same God who takes care of me will supply all your needs from his glorious riches, which have been given to us in Christ Jesus" (NLT). From my understanding of this passage, God promises to take care of our *needs*. I learned that we have needs and wants. My son came home one day from school and told me that his teacher told him that needs are more important than wants. I told him that his teacher was very correct, and since then, I have made both of my sons prioritize things before deciding on what to get or not.

In economics, the idea of survival is real, meaning someone could die if their needs were not met. *Needs* can be categorized as shelter, food, health, water, and air. *Wants*, in economics, are simply something people desire to have, which they may or may not be able to obtain.

A want is unnecessary. It is a desire that a person can live without. Life will continue if a person doesn't get what he or she wants.

Wants are also personalized. All human beings may have similar needs, but not every human being will have the same wants. A want depends on your lifestyle, background, and life perspective. Wants also vary; one person may want to own a car, and another may want to travel to an exotic country. Each person has his or her own list of wants, each with a varying level of importance.

Our wants can also change over a period of time. This is in contrast to needs, which remain constant throughout a person's lifetime.

This made me understand Philippians 4:19 in a new way; God fulfills the word in our lives as he has promised. He is a faithful God, and *all* we *need* to live, he has provided without us doing anything to justify it. Things that we don't have that we work overtime and endure sleepless night and double shifts and second jobs for are *wants*. Are those wants truly worth the stress? The reason we confuse the two so easily is that our culture teaches us to be impulsive and to listen to our urges. We are taught that you only live once (YOLO), that you should "just do it," and to enjoy the moment, but we never consider the unnecessary stress we undergo in the chase to get those things.

Now, after going through all that stress, we begin to dislike the very things we wanted. For example, have you noticed how you so wanted to have that car and you worked and did everything you could to get it, but the moment you own it and get on the road, you discover it is now common and everybody you see on the road drives the exact same car? And to make it worse, your neighbor, to whom you do not talk, bought the same car. And that church member who refuses to greet you shares the testimony of how his or her boss blessed him or her with the same car, exactly the same car you worked for, fasted for, and stressed over. The value you placed on that car diminishes to zero immediately, and you suddenly begin the race again to acquire another car.

Really? Why? Who are we trying to impress? The fellow who does not care to know your last name, who does not care how many bills you have monthly, or who does not care if you live or die?

Let it go. Lay it all down at His feet. It's not worth it at all.

I am not saying that wanting a second car or wanting a new home or wanting a new pair of shoes or a new purse is bad. Not at all. I am simply saying that we should not stress over them. We should not let our desire for them overwhelm us until we find ourselves in unnecessary illness.

If you have already prayed about and given any area of your life to the Lord but you find yourself still worrying about it, it is most likely because you have tried to take on the care of that thing by trying to deal with it on your own. Recognize that He has promised to take care of you, guide you, and provide for you, and release it over to Him once and for all.

If you find yourself worrying about that thing again, stop it right in its tracks and say, "No. I refuse to worry about this thing anymore, because God is taking care of it!" He promises that if we do this, His peace, which passes all understanding, will flood our minds as we put our trust in Him (Phil. 4:7 NLT)

Sometimes it's not what we are going through that drowns us but the way we choose to go through them.

–Bookey Itoandon

CHAPTER 9

Not the End

Have you noticed that the world has not come to an end since you've been trying so hard to perfect things in your life and around you? You put so much effort into doing things in a particular way every time, 365 days a year, seven days a week, and twenty-four hours a day, and when things don't turn out your way, you get frustrated. Perfection is an action or process of improving something until it is faultless or as faultless as possible.

But, my dear, I have realized that only God is perfect.

People will judge you no matter what as long as what you do is not according to their yardstick. You can smile or frown, sit down or stand, talk or stay silent; it doesn't matter. Some people only see negative things. When you win, they don't celebrate you, but when you are down, they show up and offer every unimaginable help. When you choose to spend time alone, they complain that you don't reach out enough, yet the moment you reach out to them, they complain about you being needy.

Some people just can't celebrate you because your victory or success didn't come from them. They don't rejoice with you when they cannot take glory for your success. Therefore, you should meditate daily on the word of God and give all the glory to him. He alone deserves it. Don't let anyone's judgment of you put you down or make you sin. God is love; that's his nature. So, love on.

I have learned to make excuses for people when I notice any strange attitude, and that has helped my spirit a lot. I tell myself things like, "He must be having a bad day," and "Whatever it is has nothing to do with me," or "She doesn't mean it. It's stress or frustration." These excuses help me laugh and overlook the situation. "We know how much God loves us, and we have put our trust in his love. God is love,

and all who live in love live in God, and God lives in them"
(1 John 4:16 NLT).

Honestly, it hurts. I can't lie about that. I cry sometimes.
Even though I try to worship through it while I shake it
off, sometimes I just pray in the spirit in an unknown
tongue, but I don't keep it bottled in and look for a coping
mechanism. That leads to bitterness, which I can't live with.

Those who know me know that I know how to talk. I
say it as I see it when I see it. I may be right or wrong, but I
say it and clear my mind of it. However, this has good and
bad effects, and I have partaken of both. What I like most
about being able to talk about things on the spot is that I
get to release it from my heart the moment it is out of my
mouth. Sometimes I'm able to make excuses for it, and
sometimes I just reply in a sarcastic way. Sometimes, I go
as far as apologizing for what I don't know, if no allegation
has been brought upon me. I discover that some people
would rather stuff it up inside, and the pain eats them up,
while the person they are unhappy with has no clue. They
seem to enjoy their life's bitterness. Bitterness is the cause

of some terminal diseases; no human being is worth me suffering over.

Plus, in my life, ever since I accepted Jesus Christ as my Lord, I get caught and pay dearly if I do what others do. People do things and get away with them, but the day I try it, I get caught. If you hurt me either through words or actions, I can't retaliate. I have tried to before, and I have landed in the hospital every time I try it. That's too much power to give anyone. No one is worth that.

There is no need to get angry, frustrated, or bitter with people when things are not done your way. "All things were made by him, and without him was anything made that was made" (John 1:3 KJV).

There is absolutely no need to be perfect, simply because you already are perfect. Striving for perfection, no matter what kind, will set you on a journey without a destination; the destination doesn't exist. I think it's important to realize that you already have everything it takes to be happy in life because the only factor that happiness depends on is *you*! It's still not the end of the world yet, so live in love and be happy! Here are the other two steps of fundamental actions I consider valuable in my attempt to love and pursue what is beneficial to me

Let Go

We should stop getting angry when people don't act the way we do or according to our expectations. What works for you may not work for me, but that doesn't make me less human. Neither does it make me an unbeliever just because our ways of living are different. In order to love yourself more, you have to start with a positive frame of mind. Accept that you are who you are, for all your ups and downs

Once you do this, you will begin to realize how others perceive your actions and learn the consequences of those actions. You learn what tasks you are and are not suited to and can then choose accordingly. You know when to stand your ground and when it simply isn't worth it. In essence, you learn who you are and what is truly at your core by letting go what isn't essential to you and figuring out what makes you tick.

I used to write a to-do list every night before going to bed—a list of things I planned to accomplish the following day, right from the moment I opened my eyes. I would pack the list full, leaving no time for rest. I just had to finish it all, and then I would feel accomplished, not worrying about the loved ones I might have trampled upon throughout the day. I would get so frustrated whenever I didn't complete my to-do list. But I remember it took God six days to create the heavens and earth and all that is in it, and then he rested on the seventh. Who am I to think I can do everything in one day, around the clock, without rest? "And God blessed the Seventh day and declared it holy, because it was the day when he rested from all his work of creation" (Gen 2:3 NLT).

Let go of all things that put you off, stress you, and get you unnecessarily worked up. Just let go!

Letting go means to hand off and release all your thoughts and imaginations to God. Accepting what you cannot change and leaving it all to God serves as the impetus for freedom. Letting go is mostly not what you think it is:

- Letting go is admitting you do not have power over the situation.
- Letting go means the outcome is not up to you.
- Letting go is accepting that you probably won't get what you want (but God is much more than enough).
- Letting go is accepting that you can't fix everything and everyone.
- Letting go means realizing that your desire to be in charge only frustrates you.
- Letting go is learning from natural circumstances.
- Letting go is not trying to fix everything but rather being an encourager.
- Letting go is not judging but allowing others to be human instead.
- Letting go is not pretending there is no problem but rather accepting it.

- Letting go is casting all your cares on the Lord.

Life will have stops along the way; some stops will be painful and some will be fun, but it's important to be grateful for all of them. Every day and everything you encounter is a gift.

It's not as though that hurt or pain never happened, but the Lord is able to take those circumstances and turn them into something beautiful in your life. If you continually live for the approval of men, you might die from their rejection.

Schedule Rest

For as long as you can remember, have you ever planned for rest? It's amazing how we create daily to-do lists of things we plan to accomplish and none of them include rest. We think resting means being lazy. I've met some people who say it as a prayer, "May I never rest," and when asked, they proudly answer that only lazy people rest because time is ticking and time waits for no one, so they need to make every minute count.

We grow up with that thinking, and we make a long list of things we must accomplish before a certain age. For example, I must be married before age twenty-five, I must own a Bentley before thirty, I must pay off my mortgage before forty, etc. All of these ambitions are great and can be realized and enjoyed if you include some time to rest in those plans. It's pointless to hustle for all of these things and then be bedridden and unable to enjoy them.

I'm sure you are telling yourself that I can't be talking about you because you take vacations yearly, but my dear, there's a difference between rest and vacation.

Vacation means a holiday and travel, while rest is a bodily state characterized by minimal functional and metabolic activities. Most of us have an activity list for when are on vacation. We respond to every call and text message we receive. Some of us still take office work along on vacation, while others feel the need to respond to every work email.

Rest as defined by the *Oxford Dictionary* as "to cause someone or something to stop doing a particular activity or stop being active for a period of time in order to relax and get back your strength."

I learned that rest means virtually shutting down for a while. It doesn't have to be long hours or days or months like a vacation, but taking a ten- or fifteen-minute rest can improve the way you function instead of just pushing yourself on and on even when your body and mind are tired. It's very helpful and refreshing.

When we face time crunches, sleep is often the first thing to get cut off. It may seem efficient and even smart at the time, but it's not. In reality, you getting that optimal sleep is going to enable you to wake up and do the job to the best of your ability.

To get more from your rest, you should try putting away most of the things that can get in the way of that rest, even if it's for thirty minutes. Put away the gadgets and smartphones. The best sleep is achieved when you turn it all off to the greatest extent that you can before bed.

You make a list of things to accomplish daily, monthly, and yearly, right? You should start including rest on that list at least for thirty minutes daily; this rest time is different from your regular bedtime at the end of the day. It's time for you to just calm down. If you choose to do it at work, you may just step away from your desk and stand by the window, looking out and gazing at nothing. It's okay to ignore the phone call; if it's important, the caller will leave a message and you can call him or her back. I realized the office won't shut down because you are sick, so you should have that at the back of your mind; they need you to be well in order to function at your optimum. If you schedule your rest time to be at home, it can be a time to just lie down and do nothing, no phone calls, no mind calculating, just gazing at the ceiling. We have routines for many things throughout the day and often have routines for how to put our children to bed, but too many of us don't have our own routines for how to shut down. We just flop into bed and hope it happens.

Worry is not of the Lord. It's a sin. It shows that you do not have complete trust in God as you profess you do. Matthew 6:34 reads, "So, don't worry about tomorrow, for tomorrow will bring is own worries. Today's trouble is enough for today" (NLT). Michael Hyatt says, "Shortchanging your sleep to get more done is actually sabotaging your success."[5]

Enjoy God!

Yes, you too can enjoy God's love, grace, and backing in your life and all you do. He already loved you right from the start, when He formed you in your mother's womb, and He longs for your love too.

When we offer ourselves to God, He sends His Holy Spirit to live within our spirits, as illustrated by the following three passages:

- "And God has given us his Spirit as proof that we live in him and him in us" (1 John 4:13 NLT)
- "We are witnesses of these things and so is the Holy Spirit, who is given by God to those who obey him" (Acts 5:32 NLT)

---

[5] Michael Hyatt, How to Harness sleep to boost your productivity, tweet quote.

- "For his Spirit joins with our spirit to affirm that we are Gods Children" (Romans 8:16 NLT)

Life is no longer about doing whatever we want. We belong to Jesus, and our bodies are the Spirit's holy temple: "Don't you realize that your body is the temple of the Holy Spirit, who lives in you and was given to you by God? You do not belong to yourself" (1 Cor. 6:19–20 NLT)

From the moment, we give our lives to God, the Holy Spirit gives us the power and desire to live for God. As we submit ourselves daily to Him, pray, read the Bible, worship, and fellowship with other Christians, we grow in our faith and in our understanding of how to please God. "Rather, you must grow in the grace and knowledge of our Lord and Savior Jesus Christ. All glory to him, both now and forever! Amen" (2 Pet. 3:18 NLT).

Jesus said, "If anyone would come after me, let him deny himself, take up his cross daily, and follow me" (Luke 9:23 NLT) Often, the path God wants for us leads in a different direction from the one we or our friends would choose. It's the choice between the broad way and the narrow way. Jesus knows the purpose for which He created us. Discovering that purpose and living it is the secret to real happiness. Following Jesus is the only way we ever find it.

You can make Jesus your Lord and Savior by simply confessing Him as your Lord in a short prayer. It is important that you accept Him in your heart and say the prayer out loud with your mouth. That means you have allowed Him to come into your heart and will make Him Lord of your life.

"That if you confess with your mouth the Lord Jesus and believe in your heart that God has raised Him from the dead, you will be saved" (Rom. 10:9 NLT).

When you love someone, you say it with your mouth, and you follow it with actions. Say this prayer:

> Lord Jesus, I realized that You are the Son of God and You came to this earth to die for my sins. Thereby, you have redeemed my life from sin and shame. I surrender all

my sins and ways of living to You, and I
hereby invite You to come into my life now.
Lord Jesus, take Your place in my heart
and be my King, my Lord, and my Savior.
From this day forward, I will no longer be
controlled by sin, or the desire to please
myself, but I will follow You all the days of
my life. My days are in Your hands, and I
pray this in Jesus's holy name. Amen.

That's all it takes. You are a new creature. You are now
born again, and all your sin and old things are gone away.
You are new.

Welcome to your new family of Christ. God loves you
so much more than you could ever know. Keep your new
relationship with Jesus alive by taking time to read His word
(the Bible) and talk to Him in your prayers daily. He loves
to hear your voice constantly, so don't be a stranger.

Remember, if what you've gained exhausts your life, it's

a loss, and if what you've lost frees your life, it's a gain. So, let it go!

Nothing can change the fact that those bad things happened, but the effect they have on you today can be changed. They can be buried, they can be left behind, they can be shed, and victory can come out of them. Good can come of it, and you can find freedom in letting those things go. It's not as though that hurt or pain never happened, but the Lord is able to take those circumstance—no matter how dark, sad, hurtful, painful, or unjust—and turn them into something beautiful in your life.

When you truly give it all to the Lord, then He is able to pour the elixir of His love, with all its healing power, into your heart in full measure. Praise God in the middle of whatever you may be experiencing. Weeping may endure for a night, but joy comes in the morning (Ps. 30:5). Your praise is the weapon you need to fight your way to a breakthrough. He can soothe, He can mend, He can heal any hurt, any pain, any past, and He will. All that He asks is that you let go.

God cannot bless who you pretend to be. So, *yes*, it is me, Olubukola Adebola Esther Attolle Itoandon (Nee Eyitayo). *Yes*, I don't know it all. *Yes*, I don't have it all. *Yes*, I can't be there for all. Yes, I had a stroke. *Yes*, God restored me through Jesus Christ. And *yes*, He can restore whatever you need Him to in your life too.

I am

S—sanctified;

T—transformed;

R—restored;

O—overcomer;

K—knowledgeable; and

E—elevated.

Every pain has a purpose. God is very intentional, and He doesn't let you go through the storm for nothing. You just have to choose to look for the good in every situation. Remember after every storm comes the Sunshine.

ABOUT THE AUTHOR

Bookey Itoandon is a Nigerian-American author, a Barrister at Law and an entrepreneur. She is very diligent and committed to her fashion business and carries out same dedication towards any assignment she is involved. She is a woman of faith, hardworking and resilient in the power of Christ.

She is very tidy and detail oriented, passionate about fashion and sketching. She is the creative designer at Attolle' Clothiers, an online fashion store she started in Houston, TX, U.S.A. She is happily married to Kelvin Itoandon and together raising two great leaders-Judah and Jedidiah Itoandon.

She now propagates the No Stress No Stroke Movement.

Follow at www.Stroke2heels.com

Printed in the United States
By Bookmasters